LESLIE W. DUNBAR

Reflections by Friends

LESLIE W. DUNBAR

Reflections by Friends

JULY 2016

NEWSOUTH BOOKS
Montgomery

NewSouth Books
105 S. Court Street
Montgomery, AL 36104

Copyright © 2016 by Tony Dunbar
All rights reserved under International and Pan-American Copyright Conventions. Published in the United States by NewSouth Books, a division of NewSouth, Inc., Montgomery, Alabama.

Publisher's Cataloging-in-Publication Data

Leslie W. Dunbar : reflections by friends
p. cm

ISBN 978-1-60306-441-5 (paperback)

I. Title.

2016950791

A hardcover edition has also been produced.

Thanks to Randall Williams for book design and production.

Printed in the United States of America

Introduction

The idea for collecting these "recollections" came from Rev. Mel Williams, formerly pastor of the Watts Street Baptist Church in Durham, North Carolina, and he guided and encouraged the contributors. He and my father would both say that the other guided and encouraged him.

— Tony Dunbar

Contents

Introduction / 5

Vernon E. Jordan, Jr. / 9
Harriet Barlow / 12
Charles Prejean / 14
Mary J. Dean / 18
Paul M. Rilling / 20
Connie Curry / 22
Mike Clark / 24
Priscilla McMillan / 30
Gordon Whitaker and Bob Hellwig / 33
Marcia Owen / 35
Mel Williams / 37
T. Evan Faulkenbury / 42
Charles Bussey / 47
Hugh Knox / 52
John Lewis / 54
Steve Suitts / 56

A Short Biography / 60
A Leslie Dunbar Reader / 63

Vernon E. Jordan, Jr.

MARCH 8, 2016

Dear Les,

I remember when you told me early in my tenure at the Southern Regional Council that if I wanted to be a leader, I had to write. It seems fitting that after more than a half century of friendship, I heed your advice once more and put pen to paper. I am writing now to tell you how blessed I have been to benefit from your mentorship, and to remind you how thankful our nation should be for your leadership.

It's hard to overstate the impact you've had on my life, as my counselor and friend. When you recruited me from the NAACP to work at the SRC in 1963, I remember I was making $5,200— and you offered me $6,500. Back then, I thought that was all the money in the world. Of course, I was happy to be making more money, but I took the job because you recognized that it was the right next step for me. And in retrospect, the greater benefit came from working alongside you.

At almost every turn, in almost every area, I've taken your advice. With one notable exception: we have very different ideas of what constitutes a relaxing vacation.

I remember in 1966 or so, you went on vacation—a drive from Atlanta to Colorado. You camped out along the way, sleeping on the ground. You told me that I should go on a similar vacation. My response: "As much as you fight for us, and as much as you give your life and time to advancing us, you really don't understand us

. . . We've been sleeping on the ground since slavery, my vacation is going to include a hotel!"

All jokes aside, you did understand the importance of ending racism, and in all your work tried to understand—and help others understand—the challenges and the humanity of the black community.

Les, not a day goes by that I don't appreciate all the good you did for me, and I hope more people come to appreciate how much good you did for this country—as a writer, an academic, an activist and a philanthropist.

I hope to do my part to make sure that America does not forget that Les Dunbar knew and worked with every leader of the movement—Dr. Martin Luther King, Jr. and John Lewis and Wiley Branton and Roy Wilkins and Dorothy Height. That we not forget your leadership continued after you left the frontlines of the South and started funding the movement through the Field Foundation. That we not forget the simple power of your perspective: the white West Virginian who cared deeply, and who took up the cause of back people because it was the right thing to do.

When we met each other, white people were not called civil rights leaders, but, Les, you have earned the right to be called a civil rights leader. And not only are you a leader, I believe you're one of the unsung heroes of the movement. And that is why I sing the ballad of Les Dunbar for anyone who will listen.

With your gentle and easy manner, you saw people—black and white, rich and poor—as they were, and your work gave them dignity and a voice. You understand the fight for civil rights has many fronts, from voter registration to school desegregation, poverty and political science, to the market and moral consequences of racism. Throughout your entire career you have built bridges between communities, and been an advocate for what you rightly called our "common interest."

At a time when our country feels divided, and when the vitriol of demagogues passes for public discourse, we need more people like you, Les. We need more people willing to fight for the rights of those who may not look like them, but who share a country and a common future.

We need to continue the work you so bravely carried forward from SRC to the Field Foundation and beyond. And as our model and guide, we still look to you.

Your friend and mentee,
Vernon E. Jordan, Jr.

Harriet Barlow

Contemplating Leslie Dunbar

Our mutual friend and colleague David Hunter was a fine stone sculptor. I have two heads by him, one of Arthur Rubenstein, the other of Jacques Costeau. David said, "If I'm going to spend scores or hundreds of hours with a man while carving his head, I want him to be both admirable and beautiful." I wish I had commissioned David to craft the head of Leslie Dunbar who certainly fulfills David's core criteria. And I'd like to have his likeness to contemplate because, like a majestic tree, I know I would never tire of it and it would help me, as Leslie helped me, to keep things simple, even as life itself and politics are not, and to trust to the truth as a lodestone.

It was David who "set me up," as he put it, with Leslie. I went to the Field Foundation office assuming my own expertise. After a long, quiet conversation, I departed realizing that what I knew, when compared to what I needed to know, would fit into a thimble. Leslie asked me an different sort of question from those I had answered in other philanthropic offices. His query excavated the provenance of my thinking. He was curious about my reading, whom I turned to as leaders in the work, how my understanding of past movements and history informed the strategies I thought promising. It was a kindly and definitive revealing of my unpreparedness. I didn't mind a bit. Only a true mentor is capable of holding up a mirror to one's inadequacy without making that deficit seem inevitable.

Over the years, when others seemed facile or their motives or approaches worried me, before intervening I reflected on that first conversation with Leslie. How did he inspire me to be more thorough, more sensibly radical, more effectively collaborative without ever saying that I was failing to be any one, much less all, of those thing? The summary notion that I've adopted, which is the core principle for facilitating gatherings at Blue Mountain Center, is that the question mark, not the exclamation point, is our punctuation of choice.

That Leslie and Peggy became part of my extended family life through Linda was the elixir that transformed a professional connection into the comfort and joy of friendship. I really don't need the sculpture. I believe I have the measure of the man to access for the remainder of my life, as I surely shall.

With love from Harriet Barlow.

Charles Prejean

Leslie Dunbar, a Genuine Force for Good

By the time I came to Atlanta, January 1968, to take the job as the executive director of the newly created Federation of Southern Cooperatives (FSC), a rural development organization for poor rural Southerners, Leslie Dunbar had already left for New York to head the Field Foundation. Though gone, I soon became aware that his footprints were all over the place, not only in Atlanta but throughout the South and then nationally.

It quickly became obvious to me that he was genuinely driven by a deep concern for the South and its people and pained over the problems they caused, inherited and sustained. He published scholarly essays and books on the social and economic conditions in the South, about its politics, poverty, race relations and the contemporary civil rights movement. He was well respected and had a seat in conference rooms of leading White progressives, as well as at public and private venues. He also sat at the tables and church pews of the Black leadership of Atlanta, the region, and the nation.

From the information that I was able to piece together over the past forty plus years, Leslie spoke "truth to power," as some of us still say, in each of these circles of society. He spoke with the same genuineness, honesty, and did so unequivocally in each case. Even his friends were not spared our blunders. Friend or foe, he spoke to, or of, with untypical gentleness and respect. I would even say that his practice of life was guided by the Christian principle of the "Servant Leader." He wrote and spoke about the wrongs in society and he did his best to correct these, all for the purpose of human betterment.

Even before meeting Leslie, I had learned much about him and his association with the Southern Regional Council. I had the good fortune to be afforded tutelage status at SRC for nearly a year. This arrangement gave me a quick study of the heritage and founding mission of SRC, its leadership, associates, and its many activities in pursuit of a more just and egalitarian society. Being the more parochial minded youngster whose community involvement efforts were limited to Louisiana, I never dreamed of being even vicariously associated with social justice giants like of the founders of Southern Regional Council and those of its predecessor organization, the Commission on Interracial Justice. What impressed me greatly was the heroic courage of these men and women during the perilous period in which they plied their efforts to seek racial and economic justice for Blacks in particular. The first half of the 20th Century South gave little quarter to those who chose to defy the strict and unrelenting canons of the segregated society.

During my apprenticeship, I came to see Leslie as the keeper of the flame of these men and women who founded the CIC, like Will Alexander, Willis Weatherford, John J. Egan and Robert Moton, and others, as well as the likes of the renowned sociologist, Howard Odum and the president of Fisk, Charles Johnson, who along with determined men and women brought forward and added to the work of the CIC with the creation of SRC. Leslie's tenure at SRC was no less necessary and dangerous and certainly as productive and beneficial as were his predecessors. The organized efforts of the CIC and SRC were not only of foundational importance to the success of the mid-century civil rights movement but also of direct importance. These men and women were fighting on the battle field for justice and equality and doing so at great risk.

I did not personally meet Leslie until the winter of 1968, at a meeting in New York with a group of foundations and organizations concerned with the unfinished business of the civil rights movement. There was particular concern for the violence in so many cities, in part precipitated by the assassination of Dr. King and what seemed to some a determined resistance to school desegregation and economic advancement. Leslie's comments at the meeting at first escaped me, given the low pitch of voice. I was expecting to hear a much more forceful sound. Somewhat bewildered, I wondered how a person who had done so much and was so involved in the quest for human justice speak so softly. I was expecting to hear a hell-raising, fist-shaking, and roof- raising person, as I had become accustomed to hear in so many church and community meetings. Needless to say as we all have learned, some who speak the loudest and often have little else to offer. Though straining to hear him, I was very pleased to hear what he had to say.

To me what was so impressive was his ability to create a framework of support and to gather allies therein to confront the ills of the South. A grant from the Field Foundation was sufficient imprimatur needed to gain support from other funding sources in the Field Foundation orbit.

I feel fortunate to claim Leslie as a friend and mentor. He has supported the work of the Federation of Southern Cooperatives from its founding and even after the closing of the Field Foundation. He willingly co-chaired, with his fellow political scientist Mack Jones, a national committee established to fight a vicious racist attack against the Federation of Southern Cooperatives in the late 1980s. This motley group of Alabama Whites had conspired to convince the U.S. Attorney for the Northern District of Alabama to investigate FSC. The reason given had to do with some vague accusation of impropriety. After nearly two years of rummaging through the FSC files and examining its records as far back as its founding (1967) and general harassment by the FBI, no impropriety was found and the investigation ended.

Though FSC knew all along that it had done nothing wrong, it still would have been presumptuous on its part to expect vindication. Help was needed to make a convincing national outcry and to garner the support needed to combat this public abuse of power. It was with Leslie's leadership and that of his co-chair, Mack Jones, that a national defense committee was created and the necessary support was found and brought to bear against this miscarriage of justice and won the day for FSC.

The gift of his friendship and that of his late wife, Peggy, will always be cherished. They welcomed us into their home and helped us to understand that human goodness resides where it pleases. It does not discriminate and we can find it more frequently than not if we look for it.

Mary J. Dean

A Loving Remembrance of Les Dunbar

My tribute to Leslie Dunbar is mostly a personal one. I met my husband Kenneth Dean when I was 21 and a junior at Mississippi College. It was not long after dating Ken that I was introduced to Les Dunbar who directed the Field Foundation at the time. He was in and out of Mississippi, doing the brave work with Civil Rights that Ken was also engaged in. Les was always supportive of both of us in extraordinary ways which I will never forget.

One day when I was driving him somewhere, he asked how I came to think the way I did and not like most other Mississippi young women. I told him I didn't know, except that I knew what was right to do, and studying literature and history critically, and meeting Ken and working with him had matured me into a decent liberal human being. Les was always so kind and warm with me, tender and caring, understanding how scared and fragile I must have seemed.

My marriage to Ken in 1967 was not met with smooth sailing within my family, as Ken's board of the Mississippi Council on Human Relations were invited, some of whom were black. My parents balked at this at First Baptist Church, Hattiesburg, so we were married in the beautiful chapel of Drew University, Madison, New Jersey, where I was a graduate student in English Literature. Les came over to the wedding from New York and shared in that celebration with us. For me, that was deeply personal gesture because I was not in my home church or with my extended family. A few years later, we named our first daughter after Leslie and Marian Wright—Leslie Marian Dean.

In August 2015, Ken and I visited Les and Tony in Leslie's retirement home in New Orleans. It was a beautiful visit, a kind of reminiscence that one hopes for toward the end of life's journey. The bright mind, the kindness and integrity, the handsome looks and distinguished demeanor had not changed at all. We felt blessed to be in his presence.

Others will be writing about the brave and bold contributions of Leslie Dunbar throughout his life, and they will know more and write more profoundly than I ever could. I will remember always the brave and bold way that Les supported all of us who were engaged in those struggles of the '60s, and how much he genuinely cared, not just about the struggle, but also about those who were risking their lives to bring about equality and justice. I am reminded of a quote from Franklin D. Roosevelt, and I believe it was, and is, Leslie's hope and prayer as well.

"If civilization is to survive, we must cultivate the science of human relationships—the ability of all peoples, of all kinds, to live together, in the same world at peace."

Blessings and love to you, Les.

Paul M. Rilling

Les Dunbar and I worked together at the Southern Regional Council in Atlanta during the late 1950s and early '60s Les was research director and then executive director of the Council during those years. In a largely behind-the-scene role Les made a significant contribution to the cause of equal justice.

SRC sought to be a "respectable" human rights agency. Its board of directors included black and white business and professional leaders from across the region. It sponsored a network of state "councils on human relations" to work at the state and local levels. SRC encouraged dialogue across racial lines, compliance with federal court rulings. It sought progress with as much cooperation and as little conflict as possible. It was termed by one black leader as "an organization of liberal whites and conservative blacks"

Les was the person we all know, modest, soft-spoken, a non-threatening demeanor, and calm under pressure. He seemed more like the academic he had been than a civil rights advocate. He brought important skills to SRC, knowledge of southern history, the ability to quickly analyze the meaning of what was happening across the region. When the student lunch counter sit-in movement began in North Carolina, within a week Les wrote a thorough report of the events and what they would mean to the non-violent resistance movement. It was one of many such papers he wrote.

Under Les SRC became a reliable source for information about the changing developments in civil rights. The information was used by academics, by other civil rights organizations and by the news media. Les frequently briefed journalists, providing the facts and suggesting what they meant. Reporters from the *New York Times* and the *Washington Post* told me they came through Atlanta on most trips South to get the latest information. Sometimes they could be given the names of persons close to developments in the places involved. Watching Les I learned that if you provide the media with accurate factual information your interpretation of the meaning of the data will often be used in their stories. These media contacts contributed to the growing, essential national support for civil rights protests in the south.

During the Kennedy administration Les was in contact with federal officials. On one occasion when I was going to Albany, Georgia, during the ongoing conflict there Les told me to call a ranking official in the federal Department of Justice and report on developments as I saw them. Les was in touch with most civil rights organizations. He sought to share information and encourage coordination among these groups. He was personally close to Dr. Martin Luther King, Jr. SRC convened regional meetings of civil rights organizations several times a year. Participating were groups such as the Friends Service Committee, the NAACP, the Urban League, SCLC and others

When HOPE, an Atlanta committee, was seeking to keep the public schools open in those early years, SRC put them in touch with leaders of an even earlier, similar group in Little Rock, Arkansas. During the New Orleans school crisis, SRC provided support and advice to two citizen groups working with the local school board to comply with federal court orders to keep public schools open.

Les had the active involvement of his board members and the one-person staffs of the state councils. Les was active in every phase of the agency's activities. He personally handled the media briefings and most contacts with heads of civil right organizations and federal officials. When he became executive director he employed a research director for his former position, but he continued to provide much of SRC's research and analysis. I served as field director for SRC until 1962 and very much enjoyed and appreciated working with Les during those important years. I learned much from the experience.

Connie Curry

I first met Les Dunbar when I moved to Atlanta in January of 1960. I was opening an office for a new project called the Southern Student Human Relations Project to bring together white and black students who were against the laws of segregation and to discuss possible campaigns and strategy to bring about change. The staff of the Southern Regional Council was helpful from the start, including finding office space for me and introducing me to the other individuals and agencies who were working for change all over the south. When Les became the SRC director in 1961, I felt I could talk with him about any problems with my project and always receive his thoughtful suggestions given in his reserved and gentle manner.

I always thought he was way ahead of many of his peers in his views on changing race relations and was aware of the respect he received from Atlanta black college and community leaders. The SRC sponsored a group called the Southern Interagency Conference and gave a wonderful opportunity for people like me to be in touch with groups all over the south who were trying to break down our segregated lives.

Hayes Mizell, a young white student in South Carolina speaks of Les and when he heard him give a talk in the '60s. "I wished I could get up and speak and tell people what I thought and have them listen. He was one of the influences that suffused my vision and aspiration."

I was so happy to read Les's *The Shame of Southern Politics*, published in 2002—such an honest description of many years of Southern politicians. I loved the title and to be able to read his essays and speeches from over many years. He remains an inspiration to me and I am happy to contribute to memories of life and work.

Speaking to the Loyal Democrats of Mississippi Convention, 1968.

Mike Clark

Good Friend Leslie,

I hope these memories, and my great affection for you, comes through in these pages. I wish I could be there with you in person to share more stories and times.

With all best wishes,
Mike Clark

APRIL 14, 2016

Looking back over 44 years of work on social change in America, I see now that Leslie has been my most strategic and consistent mentor. Carrying out such a task has not always been pleasant, but he stuck to the chore and I benefited.

Leslie and I first crossed paths in 1972 when I was on the Highlander staff in Tennessee. Frank Adams and I were overseeing the school and Leslie had just given us one of many general support grants from the Field Foundation for our program work in Appalachia. I had, of course, heard of Leslie for years as the head of the Field Foundation, one of the most liberal and fearless private foundations funding social change work in the South. Our first encounter was not a pleasant one. Frank and I journeyed to NYC to see Leslie in person so that we could share with him the news that a senior Highlander administrator had stolen the entire grant and was using it to finance a degree from a New England divinity school. Leslie took the news in good order, but his soft southern voice climbed several degrees in disbelief as we explained that the grant was gone and that we had no hope of recovering it, given the general hostility of law enforcement agencies and the courts toward Highlander in Tennessee. We shared his frustration, first in words and then in bourbon.

From that inauspicious beginning Leslie and I built a friendship that taught me many vital lessons. Soon after the first meeting I became the executive director of Highlander, a post I held for ten years and through many subsequent Field Foundation grants. Leslie, like me, was determined to find a way to deal with the many injustices in Appalachia created by the coal industry. In particular, both of us hated strip mining for coal and sought ways to have it regulated. That we failed is no surprise, but I took particular pleasure in the news that Peabody Coal Company has just filed for bankruptcy and is in serious trouble on many fronts. The company deserves all the hell it can encounter. I just wish the changes had happened when Leslie and I were working together.

Leslie taught me how to raise money from foundations, first by insisting that I had to give him a written plan laying out what we wished to do. And then by putting me through a questioning process that pushed me to clearly articulate a plan that could be measured. He always did these encounters with a courtly and gentle manner but with an insistence that logic, and not passion, be the primary source of our conversations. And his many letters to me during the grant periods were written in an elegant style, often somewhat meandering, but always ending with some hard questions that he expected to be answered. Quickly. He was a thorough teacher of policy and politics. Even if I did not realize this fact until after the conversations ended.

In the mid-seventies, I took a year off from Highlander to get married, and Deborah Tuck and I moved from Highlander to Beckley, West Virginia where she ran a UMWA sponsored housing project aimed at helping coal miners obtain ownership of their own homes—a rare idea in those areas. Leslie hired me to work for him for a year so I could take a break from Highlander duties.

Leslie and Peggy had a cabin in Renick, West Virginia, about two hours' drive from Beckley and there Leslie taught me some new lessons—how to lose in tennis and still enjoy the experience. We often played weekly at a nearby public tennis facility, and he proceeded to routinely clean me out of any winning thoughts even though he was my senior by over 20 years. On one occasion he had purchased a new racket design, an aluminum racket with a broader head. In his usual equalitarian fashion, he insisted that I use it first. With little encouragement, I beat him in three straight sets, to our mutual astonishment since the score usually went the other way. Needless to say, I went home and bought a new racket like his. In our next encounter, with matched equipment, he beat me as usual in three straight sets. Neither of us ever commented on the lessons of that process. But we had good food and bourbon to celebrate the times together.

One memorable trip taught me a great deal about Leslie and how he dealt with people and the world. We journeyed to New Mexico and Montana together to visit opponents of surface mining for coal in the West. Field had funded the National Indian Youth Council and they were working with Navajo people opposing the Four Corners Power Plant and coal mining on Navajo lands. We visited Kayenta and then went to Farmington, New Mexico, to look at the power plant and visit local activists. Our first day in Farmington saw us at a motel in town with little to do after dinner. It was summer with plenty of light left in the sky. We decided to explore the back roads around Farmington and soon found ourselves in a remote area as the sun disappeared. Traveling down a winding road in the dust, we saw up ahead a set of red lights blinking in the bushes and we heard a loud roar. Upon reaching the site, we found an older, long-hooded Cadillac pointing away from the road and buried up to its hubcaps in deep sand. Streams of dust and sand and gas fumes were pouring out of the back end, but the car was mired to its axles. Leslie braked to a halt (he always insisted on driving since the foundation was paying for the rental car and I was along, literally, for the ride) and we clambered out. Upon reaching the stranded car, Leslie began a leisurely conversation with the lone driver and they reluctantly agreed that the car was not moving out of the sand dune. The driver slowly fought his way out of the tilted car and it became immediately clear that he was also tilted under the heavy weight of alcohol. Upon further gentle questioning by Leslie, we learned that the driver was on his way to see relatives but had misjudged the road at a slight turn. To my dismay, since I have had considerable time spent with similarly tilted drivers, Leslie asked if we could help the traveler find his relatives in the dark. He quickly agreed and with a mutual waving of arms, and peering into the distance, we moved down the country road, pausing at various driveways and crossroads, until we encountered a familiar driveway. We helped him to the front of a traditional hogan and then, at my insistence, Leslie and I disengaged with the traveler and made our way back to our car and, over the next hour, retraced our tracks to a hard road and found our motel. Throughout the time, Leslie worried about our new friend and hoped that we had left him at the right hogan. I had few doubts but had begun to realize that with Leslie, any encounter, no matter how bizarre, had to be attended to carefully, in a courtly manner, and with great attention to the wishes of anyone in distress.

The next day brought more lessons. We had arranged to meet the local activists at their downtown office early in the morning. But after two hours of waiting at their door with no sign of anyone, we decided to proceed on our own to Fruitland, a few miles out in the country and near the Four Corners Power Plant where we planned to visit a local activist who was a plaintiff in a law suit that the foundation was supporting. Leslie driving, of course, we proceeded to Fruitland, a small village of tribal people. No signs, no mailboxes, no way to know where to go. Ahead of us a lone woman, dressed in traditional long skirt and headscarf, walked down the road carrying a bundle. Leslie pulled alongside, commented on the lovely morning, and said we were looking for a someone, perhaps a neighbor, a lady named Emma Yazzie?

"I am Emma Yazzie!" she said firmly. We gathered her into the car and proceeded down the road to her homestead which included a traditional hogan, small sheds, a corral with a horse inside, and a herd of sheep milling around the hillside. Beyond her home, perhaps two miles away, loomed the massive hulk of the Four Corners Power Plant. We spent the next two hours with her, slowly learning her life story as she moved around the homestead and took us inside the hogan. Now a grandmother, a weaver, a traditional person, and a sheepherder, she had been a WAC in WWII and returned to Navajo Country to take up again a traditional life. She objected to the coming of the coal mines and the power plant and had joined the law suit because of the foul air emitted by the power plant and because her sheep became sick from the fumes and the emissions. Her flock of sheep moved around us. Most of the adults were bleeding from their nostrils. After a slow and mellow and memorable telling of her story, she announced that she had to begin the day's work. We went to the corral, she saddled and mounted the horse, sent us off with many gestures and smiles, and herded the sheep into the desert country. Her presence stayed with both of us for many years. And this encounter with her was typical of how carefully, artfully, Leslie dealt with people no matter their background, their education, or their attitudes. He was courtly, gentle, inquiring and respectful. And he always gave people space to be themselves without insisting that he deserved anything other than a bit of time.

There are lots more stories about Leslie, but these will do for the moment. I have not forgotten these encounters, or the lessons, or the good times with Leslie that we have shared in both cities and countryside. In Navajo Country. In the coalfields of Eastern Montana. In the rolling hills and hollows of Appalachia. And in the elegant Field Foundation office mansion in NYC. At his home in the suburbs. And I know of no one who has moved so gracefully and carefully through the field of social change on so many fronts, from civil rights to human rights, from poverty issues to questions of war and peace, from coal mines to cotton fields, to ghettoes of our cities and of our minds. At the Field Foundation, Leslie, Ruth Field, and their colleagues, taught us how wealth and power and leverage can be used to advance common goals for society, rather than to see wealth used only for those who already possess it. These are vital, important lessons. He crafted a wonderful legacy of friendship, of hope, of strategic investments in people, of a steel will—skillfully used.

I am deeply grateful for these experiences, and for the wonderful friendship that Leslie and I share over so many years. I miss these exchanges. Our paths have separated due to my own movement to the West and now his movement to New Orleans. But he remains in my mind a great friend and a legendary force in our community's effort to create a viable dream of equality and justice for all Americans.

With all best wishes,
Mike Clark, Bozeman, Montana

Priscilla McMillan

In 1966 my husband, George McMillan, and I, were living in Atlanta, where George was teaching journalism at historically black Clark College. "I'm not one of those damned white liberals," George would say to his students. "I'm not making any sacrifice. I am paid well to stand here and lecture to you."

That George had been hired to train black newspapermen was the brain child of Leslie Dunbar, who realized that the civil rights demonstrations that were roiling the country at that time ought to be covered by black reporters and not solely by whites.

I heard a lot about Les Dunbar during those years in Atlanta. What I heard most about was the way in which he, more than anyone, had shaped national coverage of the civil rights movement by meeting with reporters from both the north and south and, in his quiet, understated way, explaining the background of each crisis as it unfolded. By the mid-'60s, Leslie's stature was such that he had moved to New York to be director of the Field Foundation, an organization that was interested in civil rights and social experiment. It was in that capacity that he had provided funds for my husband to train black journalists, as well as for countless other projects. Besides making grants for the Field Foundation, Leslie was an advance scout: if one of his projects worked out well, the giant Ford Foundation would go in behind him and follow up with a larger grant.

I remember a steamy summer evening in Frogmore, South Carolina, when Leslie brought a distinguished child psychiatrist to our house for dinner. He was Dr. Milton Senn of Yale, a man who appeared just as open to new approaches as Les. The conversation that night revolved around children. Did braving police lines and flash bulbs to integrate a school damage a young child psychologically? The psychiatrist Robert Coles, whose work, it turned out, had been subsidized by Field, insisted in his book "Children of Crisis," that not only the child but his or her entire family might benefit from being pioneers of the movement. My husband, on the other hand, had written about a family in Clinton, Tennessee, in which the child had been damaged emotionally and his family destroyed. What I remember of the evening's conversation is the quiet rumble of Leslie's voice and the depth of his concern over the impact of the civil rights struggle on individual blacks themselves.

That after moving to Durham in the 1980s, he decided to run for School Board, makes perfect sense. He had been around politics all his life, urging some candidates to run, helping others to polish their speeches. He himself had given speeches and written books, but he wasn't really the Ivory Tower type. When he saw something that needed fixing, he would do what he could to fix it.

Years later I saw Leslie in a very different setting. He and Peggy had moved to Washington to be near their daughter Linda. They were in an independent living facility on Military Road. Leslie was just the same as in the old days: he hadn't been in the place long, but already he was its leading spirit. It wasn't a civil rights crowd, but a diplomatic one, retired Foreign Service officers and their wives, and Leslie seemed perfectly at home. With a new friend named Zig Nagorsky, he and Peggy served Meals on Wheels most days; he walked to his favorite bookstore, Politics and Prose, to reminisce with the co-owner, Carla Cohen, an old friend from the sixties; and, when there was a big event on the Mall, a demonstration or an Inauguration, he walked there not wanting to miss the excitement.

While citing the jobs Leslie held over the years, I haven't mentioned that he was constantly traveling, attending demonstrations and speaking at colleges and every sort of gathering. The speeches he gave and his essays comprised at least four books, and most of the essays appeared first in the Virginia Quarterly Review. In his most recent book, "As the South Lies Dying," published less than two years ago, Leslie brought together many of the concerns of his long and active life: racism, militarism, inequality, capital punishment, the power of corporations. That he could tie so many disparate things together, and in such a cogent way, is proof of the depth with which he saw everything around him.

Let's hope that Leslie keeps writing books and articles, sharing his wisdom with the rest of us.

Gordon Whitaker and Bob Hellwig

Bob Hellwig and I met Leslie in 1992 soon after we joined Watts Street Baptist Church. Leslie quickly became an essential guide and friend, shaping our lives toward peacemaking and deepening our connection to the church. Serving with him on the Peace and Reconciliation Mission Group was a formative experience for me. Seeing and hearing his quiet, unassuming leadership gradually demonstrated to me how important close and careful listening are to guiding a group to consensus. Leslie also demonstrated the power of holding firmly to basic values while remaining open to learning what courses of action might help further them. He holds a deep commitment to honoring everyone's basic humanity and to working for justice—especially justice for those most oppressed by society. What a gift!

Quiet Sunday afternoons with Leslie and Peggy were another gift to Bob and me. We lived only about a mile from them and were invited frequently to join them for conversation, some Scotch and snacks, and—in season—inspection of Leslie's tomato plants.

Of course, Leslie's most important gifts were to the broader community. He helped focus many of our Peace and Reconciliation activities on issues of racial justice and on nonviolence. With Leslie's help Watts Street Baptist Church began marking the third Sunday of January by inviting a guest preacher to challenge us with the continuing relevance of the life and ministry of Martin Luther King. Leslie saw the importance of making this a community-wide event and extending the day to include lunch and discussion with the preacher with the broader community, too. Now, years after Leslie left Durham, the annual MLK Sundays at Watts Street Baptist Church continue to focus attention on injustices and inspire us to action.

Another of Leslie's gifts to our community is the Religious Coalition for Nonviolent Durham. Durham was plagued by violence, especially gun violence, in 1992. Leslie played a pivotal role in founding RCND to campaign for the control of handguns and to mourn publically the loss of life to violence. Leslie engaged Marcia Owen in organizing public vigils with the families of murder victims at the spots where they were killed. Unfortunately, the guns and the killing continue in Durham, but so do RCND and the vigils against violence. Under Marcia's continuing leadership RCND has expanded its work to prevent violence and to offer hope and healing with the spirit that Leslie helped instill in it.

Marcia Owen

The Joy of an Ethical Life

It is a delight to share my love and gratitude for Leslie Dunbar. I met Leslie in 1993 in response to escalating gun violence in my city of Durham, North Carolina. Our hospital emergency rooms were treating about 150 people a year for gunshot wounds. At least every other week someone was killed in Durham with eighty percent of the victims dying from gun violence. Both victims and those arrested for their deaths were overwhelmingly African-American citizens, especially young men.

In response to this suffering Leslie and his pastor, Rev. Mel Williams of Watts Street Baptist Church, had formed the Religious Coalition Against Gun Violence the previous year. Leslie and Mel were already leading a movement in Durham to strengthen policies that discouraged the proliferation of firearms and increased the responsibilities of gun ownership. The coalition grew and local ordinances were passed. Editorial boards were engaged and local reporters were offered policy, health, and criminal justice information and resources. Public health officials and private doctors joined our efforts and gun violence prevention was officially deemed a public health priority. Most importantly, the coalition began holding public prayer vigils after homicides to honor the victims, to offer comfort and resources to their families, friends and neighbors, and to bear witness to the peace among us.

Leslie created a legacy in Durham that challenged citizens and lawmakers alike to consider before making any decision how might their advocacy and their actions affect the most vulnerable neighbors of their community. He created a legacy of building uncommon relationships created from common lament and with common purpose. He created a legacy that recognized the violence of indifference.

Leslie showed me the joy of an ethical life. He taught me that values are the verbs of God. I am eternally grateful for Leslie's friendship, leadership, and for revealing to me the difference between the love of justice and the justice of love. I hope to honor Leslie's legacy by continuing to serve the Religious Coalition for years to come.

MARCH 18, 2016

Mel Williams

A Tribute to Leslie Dunbar—
"agitator" for justice and peace

My relationship with Les Dunbar began in 1988 when he joined the church in Durham where I served as pastor. At that time I knew only a little about his reputation. He was first my parishioner, but soon he became mentor and guide and eventually my friend.

With his quiet manner, Les has always seemed reluctant to reveal his role in the national movement for civil rights, peace, and economic justice. His story remains largely untold, and I hope that this collection of reflections will bring to light the significant contribution that he has made.

Leader behind the scenes

In my many conversations with Les, I've worked hard to elicit from him the leadership he has given. He finally agreed to tell me that in 1961, when he was director of the Southern Regional Council, he went with Martin Luther King, Jr., to integrate the first restaurant in Atlanta. He introduced Dr. King to Ralph McGill, then editor of the Atlanta Constitution. Les was one of a few whites in the inner circle of strategists for the Civil Rights Movement. He was personal friends and colleagues with King and most other black leaders of the movement. (Les's papers from the Southern Regional Council are now archived at Emory University.)

Leader in civil rights

Even with his writings, speeches, and leadership, Les's contribution remains under-acknowledged. Here is a phenomenal example of his untold story. In 1961 as leader of the Southern Regional Council, Leslie Dunbar wrote a 48-page document titled "The Federal Executive and Civil Rights." It was widely distributed in the US Justice Department and the Kennedy Administration.

Given his academic background in political science, in this document Les compiled a long list of actions that President Kennedy could take to move the country through the difficult days of protest and unrest. It was a kind of blueprint of action items that foreshadowed the 1964 Civil Rights Act and the 1965 Voting Rights Act. When I asked Les about the role that this document played, he muttered, "It just stated what they already had decided to do." This was a characteristic Leslie understatement.

LEADER IN THE CHURCH

When Les moved to Durham in 1988, he became a leader at Watts Street Baptist Church. Most people here did not know of his national leadership in civil rights, hunger, and peace. At our church's annual Martin Luther King, Jr. worship service, Les was instrumental in securing such notable preachers as Congressman John Lewis, Vernon Jordan, Will Campbell, Julius Chambers, and Sam Cook.

At these services at Watts Street, we heard John Lewis say, "Les Dunbar gave me my first job." Vernon Jordan said, "Where Les leads, I follow." Will Campbell described Les as "a brilliant, Lincolnesque Southerner who gave up a career in university teaching to devote his life to peaceful solutions to complex problems." Sam Cook, the first African American professor at Duke University, said that Les "was one of the principal architects of the Civil Rights Movement." Sam's assessment remains virtually unknown.

As a churchman Les has been rooted in faith and the biblical call for justice and peace. When he was a member of Watts Street Baptist Church, he was an active leader in our Peace and Reconciliation

Mission Group, where he took the initiative to encourage various community-wide events—a forum on peace at the outbreak of the Gulf War, a forum on violence and the criminal justice system. At one of the MLK services. Les kindly accepted my invitation to preach. In his sermon he quoted Jesus's mission statement in Luke 4: "The Spirit of the Lord is upon me, because the Lord has anointed me to bring good news to the poor . . . " Les commented, "This was Jesus's opening announcement, what he said would be his ministry. This is the platform from which he never departed. If we are going to bother to call ourselves his church, I think it must be our platform." (This sermon was later published in *Politics, Morality, and Higher Education: Essays in Honor of Samuel DuBois Cook*, edited by F. Thomas Trotter, p. 91)

Leader in the Durham community:

Les practiced what he preached. He quietly served as a volunteer *ad litem* with a young man who had committed some crime. (I was riding with him one day when he stopped at a public housing project and pulled a basketball goal from his car trunk, a gift for his *ad litem* youngster.) His work was not only person-to-person, but also community-wide. He ran for the Durham School Board. And one can only wonder how the School Board might have been different had he been elected.

Les also was the instigator for a new organization to stop gun violence in Durham. In 1991 over lunch, Les asked me, "Will you help organize the faith community to work against gun violence?" I eagerly joined him, and the result was the creation of a vigorous Religious Coalition for a Nonviolent Durham (RCND), led by Marcia Owen, a tireless "Mother Teresa" whom Les brought on board as the first and only executive director. Twenty-five years later, RCND continues to be a force for reducing gun violence, bringing healing and advocating for restorative justice in Durham

Leader in the Nation

At the Field Foundation, Les called together a team of physicians to go to Mississippi to document child malnutrition there. Among those Les recruited for the delegation was Dr. Robert Coles of Harvard. Peter Edelman, who served as assistant to Attorney General Robert Kennedy, wrote "The Field Foundation was run by a taciturn, deeply principled southerner named Leslie Dunbar." He also secured an early grant for Marian Wright Edelman as she began the Children's Defense Fund in Washington, D.C. Les's papers from his Field Foundation years are now archived at the University of Texas in Austin.

In his 2012 book, *Looking for the Future: A Meditation on Political Choice*, Les reflected on the inequalities that continue to abound. "There will be lots of unrest in our near future, here and in the other societies of the world where there is large private wealth held by a small minority . . . As with reforms of the 1930s, mid-'50s, the '60s and '70s, the time for unrest has arrived."

Part of Les's legacy is his call to harness the energies of the "unrest" and continue to work for nonviolence and justice. He implored us to stay involved in the ongoing movement.

"The old trilogy was liberty, equality, and fraternity, and the third I think may be chief of all . . . a call to find our own way of living in sisterhood and brotherhood with those with whom we share this time and planet. There is no more worthy ideal."

Mentor and Guide

No doubt, Les has influenced many of the ministers who have met him, and he has certainly had a major influence on my ministry. One day he and I were talking about the warring tendencies of our nation. He turned and said, "The major question is: How does any war affect the poor?" That question has become a guiding principle in my current work with End Poverty Durham. How does any policy or action or military decision affect the poor? Too often, elected decision makers are out of touch with those who struggle with poverty. Les's question has helped turn my vocational focus to economic justice, linked to persistent racial inequities.

Agitator

Les did not like the word "activist." I once asked him if that term fit him, and he said "no." I kept pushing him, and I asked, "Would you consider yourself an agitator?" With lowered voice he said, "That's a better word." Martin King referred to himself as "a drum major for justice." Standing in the background was a reserved, yet forceful Leslie Dunbar—"an agitator for justice."

Leslie Dunbar with Hillary Clinton at the White House, "FDR Reception," 1997.

T. Evan Faulkenbury

"How Leslie Dunbar Learned Race"

I first met Leslie W. Dunbar only through his voice. In 1978, he sat for a three and a half hour interview with Dr. Jacquelyn Dowd Hall for the Southern Oral History Program. I first listened to it and read along for a class assignment in Dr. Hall's "Introduction to Oral History" seminar during the spring of 2013. Later, I found another interview with Dunbar by Dr. Robert R. Korstad from 1992. Dunbar had played an important role in the civil rights movement as the executive director of the Southern Regional Council (SRC), a civil rights research agency based in Atlanta. These interviews provided a wealth of information for my dissertation research. But I heard and read something else in these interviews, something unexpected. I learned how Leslie Dunbar learned race.

Leslie Dunbar was born on January 27, 1921 in Lewisburg, West Virginia to Marion and Minnie Lee Crickenberger Dunbar. They were white, working-class people whose family roots stretched back for generations in rural West Virginia, but the Dunbars moved to Baltimore in 1930 after Leslie's father fell on hard times with the coming of the Great Depression. Leslie grew up in Baltimore, a city on the Mason-Dixon border. "Baltimore was strictly segregated in every respect," Dunbar told Korstad, "from the schools to residential areas to swimming pools and everything else. We even had in the parks, black baseball diamonds and white baseball diamonds." Although he grew up in a racially stratified environment, segregation and its consequences did not weigh on Dunbar's mind as an adolescent. "You became aware of it [segregation]," Dunbar recalled, "but not in the sense that you felt it was something you needed to do something about. We just saw the order of things."

After he finished high school, Dunbar attended the University of Maryland and went on to earn a PhD in political science at Cornell University in 1948. His first job was at Emory University, and soon after he arrived in Atlanta, his department assigned him to mentor undergraduates in its political science club. In both his interviews with Hall in 1978 and Korstad in 1992, Dunbar pinpointed one evening with the political science club that opened his eyes to racism in the American South.

"I'm not a person who has great dramatic things happen to him," Dunbar began his story to Hall. "I don't think I could ever be converted on a road to any Damascus. So I don't want to give you the wrong impression about this story I'm about to tell you."

Dunbar was in charge of bringing guests to speak to the political science club, and he decided to invite an African American professor from Atlanta University for one meeting. Dr. William Boyd held a PhD from the University of Michigan and was a noted scholar on international relations. But Dunbar did not think to ask Boyd to talk about his expertise, instead inviting him to talk to the Emory political science club about race relations in the South. Boyd agreed, and "he began telling them what it was to be a black man in the South. He began describing what he and his family went through when they drove to Washington—how you had to know where to stop, how you had sometimes to go to the woods . . . I sat there, and I heard all this, and I just had never thought of it before. I really hadn't."

Dunbar knew he had made a mistake. He should have asked Boyd to talk about international relations and not assume that because he was black, he would want to talk about race. He apologized to Boyd and all was forgiven, but Boyd opened up to Dunbar after the meeting. Boyd told Dunbar that an elephant at the Atlanta Zoo had passed away, and that his daughter's elementary school had taken up a collection to help buy another one. His daughter did not know that African Americans were not allowed at the zoo. "How do we tell our daughter that she can't go see that elephant once it's bought?" Boyd asked Dunbar. The scales fell from Dunbar's eyes, but he was ashamed that it had taken so long. "It suddenly dawned on me that he hadn't said a single thing that I needed to hear," Dunbar remembered. "I could have figured out for myself if I'd ever given it one moment's thought. If I had ever asked myself what a black man has to endure driving his family north, I could have figured out every bit of that scenario. But I'd never done that. He hadn't told me a thing that I needed to be told."

Having grown up in Baltimore, Dunbar had seen racial divides, but he had not considered the personal injustices of segregation. Boyd made it real to Dunbar. From then on, race was on Dunbar's mind. While in Atlanta, he befriended white and black civil rights activists, including the leadership of the SRC. The SRC was one of the oldest interracial organizations in the South that researched and advocated for better race relations, and Dunbar was drawn to its progressive ideals. In 1951, he left Emory University for a job at the Atomic Energy Commission, then went on to teach political science at Mount Holyoke College. He kept in touch with his friends at the SRC, and after working at its Atlanta headquarters during the summer of 1957, he accepted a job offer to lead the SRC's research division. He moved back to Atlanta in January 1958, and in 1961, he became the SRC's executive director. Until he left in 1965, Dunbar oversaw the SRC as it became a crucial ally of civil rights organizations through research, funding, and by providing a meeting place between groups.

I must have read these interviews more than a dozen times before I decided to fly to New Orleans and meet Leslie Dunbar for myself. I went for two reasons: to interview him for my dissertation research, and to hear more about the story about William Boyd.

Something about the way he told it had touched me. I could not quite put my finger on it. Maybe it was his vulnerability about his naïveté, or about the chain of events that came after. Perhaps it was the simple fact that he came to see racism in a way that many white southerners never did, or never would. But I knew that I wanted to meet him.

I had gotten in touch with Dunbar's son, Tony, who told me that his father lived in a retirement home in New Orleans. He said his father's memory was as sharp as ever, but that he was physically weak. At 92 years-old, I expected no less, but Tony encouraged me to visit him and said his father would be happy to talk. We picked a day in June 2014, I bought my plane tickets, and I planned to visit Dunbar's home for one afternoon. I prepared my list of questions, tested my recording equipment, and read his interviews one last time.

The day began with a plane delay. My flight out of Raleigh-Durham was late, and I missed my connection to New Orleans. Instead of arriving during the late morning with plenty of time to get to Dunbar's home, I did not get into New Orleans until late that evening. My flight out of New Orleans was around nine the next morning, and I worried that I had missed my chance to meet Dunbar. Tony asked his father if I could visit early the next morning before my flight, and he agreed. I showed up around seven in the morning prepared for a speedy interview.

Tony had warned me, but I had not really listened. Dunbar sat on an easy chair next to his bed with the *New York Times* laid out on a table. He was checking baseball scores, specifically for the Baltimore Orioles. He looked up when I walked in and offered me a strong handshake, although I could feel that it was a struggle. His voice was low, almost inaudible, and he had to rest for several seconds after every few words. I put away my audio equipment, and he, Tony, and I talked for about forty-five minutes. I told him about my research, about my interest in the SRC, and he shared with me a few words about certain people and events that came to mind. I showed Dunbar some photographs I discovered in the archives, and we talked about the significance of his work at the SRC. I wish we could have talked longer.

I never asked him about his encounter with William Boyd and his story of racial awakening. Maybe I should have, but I did not see the point. He had told the story twice already in separate interviews, and I did not want to exhaust him during my limited time. But I saw and met a man whose life had changed some sixty years before, who understood racial prejudice after a colleague explained it in a personal way. Dunbar learned race in 1948. Today, many still have yet to learn the lesson.

Charles Bussey

There Are No More Leslie Dunbars

On a clear, brilliant October day in 1989, my life changed. An old friend from earlier days in Kentucky, Anne Roosevelt, had invited me to a conference on "The Future of American Liberalism" at Hyde Park, New York. In the middle of the conference, the Franklin & Eleanor Roosevelt Institute made its annual presentation of the Four Freedoms Awards to persons who exemplified the ideals set forth in FDR's famous speech.

Anne and I walked through the courtyard of FDR's Episcopal Church in Hyde Park after the awards ceremony when suddenly she called out with some urgency, "Hey, Leslie!" And to me she said, "That's Leslie Dunbar. You've got to meet him."

She introduced me to an erect, gray-haired man, and we chatted for no more than five minutes. It was a rather difficult conversation, for although I didn't know it at the time, Leslie has a distinct way of conversing. Sometimes there are long pauses. And he speaks softly. I didn't have clue who he was, but I remember using the words populist and progressive in our brief conversation. "I can't use those words," Leslie said, "don't know what they mean. I'm a liberal, and that's good enough for me."

Later Anne told me that Leslie was a social justice activist and had run the Field Foundation in New York City. She knew him from his service on the FERI board, which she served then as vice president. Anne praised Leslie and said, "There are no more Leslie Dunbars." And that was the end of it. I thought.

Returning to Kentucky and my teaching duties at Western Kentucky University, Leslie kept returning to my mind, so I wrote him a letter and then called him. In the course of things, he asked me to review a book for *Southern Changes*, where he served as book review editor. I agreed. He was fun to talk to, so mentally alert and so committed to social justice, that I decided to "check him out" in the library and see what I could find. And that was a lot!

He had a Ph.D. in political science from Cornell but no undergraduate degree. After a brief stint teaching at Mount Holyoke College, he moved South to work with the Southern Regional Council, first as director of research and from 1961 to 1965 as executive director. In 1965 he moved to New York City to run the Field Foundation where he stayed until he resigned in 1980 on a matter of principle.

Still, most intriguing to me was our first brief conversation about words. "I'm a liberal. That's enough for me." Two years later Leslie sent me a copy of his 1991 book, *Reclaiming Liberalism*. It's a big little book that covers a variety of subjects from the Southern civil rights movement, which demonstrated the power of love, to militarism, to the horror of state violence in war and in implementing the death penalty. Through that book, Leslie taught me the failure of military power to bring peace, the linkage between poverty and militarism, and the need to harness the power of the state. It is a telling analysis of contemporary America and the dangers of both the American civil religion and the tremendous disparity of wealth between the haves and the have nots. In fact, in the first full paragraph on page 181, he prophetically wrote,

> We of the Industrial West . . . are much concerned about "terrorism." Terrorists are the enemies of order, of civility. Considering these conditions, the question becomes: Why should they not be?

In subsequent letters and phone conversations, Leslie continued what amounted to me private tutorials about the way a citizen should behave, what a patriot rather than a nationalist was called to do.

From January to June 1992, I found myself in Denmark as a senior Fulbright lecturer on "U.S. History Since 1945." One of my brightest Danish students, Lone Jessen, wrote a seminar paper on the "American Civil Religion" after reading Leslie's book. She was so excited. "Reading this," she told me, "is like listening to this man speak. I hope I can meet him someday."

Returning to the USA, I continued to learn from and about Leslie. I learned about his work with Martin Luther King, about the failure of the Kennedy administration to heed his advice in "The Federal Executive and Civil Rights," and about his other important work in the areas of civil rights and poverty once he moved to the Field Foundation in 1965.

In May 1995, I stopped by Leslie's home in Durham, North Carolina, where I met his wife Peggy and spent two days just listening and learning from him. It was fun, too! He cooked an incredible red beans and rice dinner and served the best martinis I've ever tasted. There, in his basement, he showed me a copy of a paper written by John Lewis dated 1966. "It's something I'm proud of," Leslie said. When Lewis had been essentially deposed at SNCC, Leslie made him a Field Foundation Fellow where Lewis wrote the paper qualifying him for a degree from Nashville's Fisk University.

Five days after my North Carolina trip, I left for a summer in NYC for an institute at David Rothman's Center for the Study of Society and Medicine at Columbia University. My former Danish student, Lone Jessen, had moved to New York to work at the United Nations, and in time married a New York businessman Jim Elkind. Upon my arrival, they treated me regularly to dinners and parties.

On June 8th Leslie tracked me down at Columbia. He was in the city for a board meeting of the Winston Foundation for World Peace. He invited me for lunch at the Wales Hotel. Coincidentally

Lone and Jim were having a birthday party for me that day at their apartment at 99th and Riverside Drive. I knew they'd be happy to have Leslie, but would he come?

When we met, I told him about the party, and he seemed pleased. "Let's walk for a while," he said, "and then get a cab up to Riverside Drive." We wandered along Madison Avenue for about 20 blocks, stopping once for a beer, as he talked about his years in NYC. He asked why I was there, and I explained about the Institute and David Rothman. "Good God!" Leslie exclaimed. "I funded one of David's early projects, a study of Willowbrook."

The party was fun with lots of salmon, smoked mackerel, cheeses, plates of fruit, and good wine as we looked out the window at the Hudson River from the 9th floor. The hosts and Leslie were deep in conversation. All shared a passion for world peace and an abhorrence for violence.

The next day I told David Rothman that Leslie Dunbar said hello. "My God!" he said. "I'd lost track of Leslie. I can't believe you know him. I was at his 60th birthday party. Super Bowl Sunday. Calvin Trillin was there. Now how the hell did Leslie know Calvin. Maybe it was Alice."

I told David how much Leslie had taught me. He laughed and started a Rothman monologue. "I'm a New York Jewish intellectual with an ego," he said, "but in the presence of Leslie Dunbar, I'm a humble man." He talked about the grant funding Willowbrook. "Every two or three months," David said, "Sheila [Rothman's wife and fellow writer] and I would go down to Leslie's office on Park Avenue. Not because we had to but because we wanted to go. He was busy as hell, you know, running a foundation. He has an enormous conscience and is a very smart man. He wasn't all that interested in intellectual issues. More the political angle. How to make life better for people cut out of the system." I tried to interrupt but failed. "I don't mean to sound corny," David said, "but Sheila and I went to see Leslie to be energized, to be challenged, to be encouraged. I mean, this is corny, but Leslie was our lodestone, our compass, our inspiration. There was an intangible quality to Leslie. He lifted us up, made us feel like we could contribute to society."

That's what Leslie has meant to me too. He's helped me become more that I ever thought I could be. He changed my life and continues to inspire and teach. About a year ago, he sent me a copy of *As the South Lies Dying: Its Dueling Legacies*, a collection of some of his essays. All he wrote was: "Charles—What is the news? Les D." Anne Roosevelt's words from the 1989 October day at Hyde Park are as clear in my mind today as the sky was then—"There are no more Leslie Dunbars."

Hugh Knox

To Leslie,

After leaving home for college an earnest but naïve white boy from New England, I soon became engaged in anti-military and pro civil rights groups like AFSC, FCNL, SNCC, CORE, the NAACP, and the MOBE, much to my parents' chagrin.

But then, after fifteen years, I met Linda and through her you and Peggy (and Tony) on a Thanksgiving weekend in Renick, West Virginia. What a treat to discover a couple with whom my views were met with positive interest. I was a generation behind!

Since 1974, we have celebrated holidays in Renick, Pelham, at Ingleside, on Drummond, in Durham, at our Kenwood House, and in New Orleans. The cast had a core, including you and Peggy, Tony and family, Nancy, Linda and family, Nha, and my family, and soon a joint family of Linda's and mine. Plus Zeb, Fritz, Pushkin, Parker, Sparky, Rascal and Topper.

Seeing that our professional lives did not mix back then, I did not realize or appreciate your eminence as a white man in a mostly black world. I now join the choir of voices heard elsewhere in this set of remembrances.

A couple of my remembrances: You and I and Jack Mathison were standing at the Washington Monument at a vigil protesting the Iraq War and I got the idea to give you a Washington Nationals baseball cap hoping to temper your love of the Orioles. The cap had what we in D.C. refer to as the "curly W." I didn't see you wear that cap for years. Turns out you thought it was a sign of support for "dubya."

The second: Seeing Linda come back from a phone call from Marian Wright Edelman asking her if she would be interested in researching and writing a book on the plight of the children of migrant workers on the east coast and did she know and could she work with another person who had been recommended—Tony Dunbar. The book got done and I have always suspected your fine hand behind that.

So here's to you, Leslie. Slainte mhath!

"For a' that, an' a' that,
Its comin' yet for a' that.
That Man to Man, the world o'er
Shall brothers be for a' that."

John Lewis

May 26, 2016

To Les Dunbar:

Please allow me to join with others in honoring you for your outstanding service and support for social justice and educational opportunities for young people in Georgia and throughout the world. Your steadfast commitment to equal opportunity and assisting those in need has helped to make Georgia and the nation a better place.

Fifty years ago, the world was a very different place. I vividly remember first meeting you; I could feel the momentum of change moving through the room. It was exciting and inspiring. You have always been a man of high character; through your work with the Southern regional Council and the Field Foundation, you helped to instill in me the importance of hard work, public service and the American dream.

When you were involved with the Southern Regional Council you served as an exemplary leader and supporter in changing racial attitudes in the South. It took nothing short of raw courage for participants in the movement to stand up to local opposition, to the governors and to the federal government.

You taught me to accept challenges with optimism and confidence and produce innovative and substantive results. Your work with SRC was instrumental in the creation of the Voter Education Project, helping to secure and distribute funds to national and local civil rights groups across the country. You encouraged us, not only to open our eyes and take notice of the injustices around us, but to take action and get involved. We became a circle of trust, a band of brothers and sisters. It didn't matter whether you were black or white. It didn't matter whether you came from the North, to the South, or whether you were a Northerner or Southerner. We were one.

Perhaps the greatest and most timeless gift of this history is that it serves as a reminder that we can make a difference. No matter how fierce our adversary, no matter how organized the opposition, no matter how entrenched the power base, nothing can stop the movement of a disciplined, determined people. Today we are standing on the shoulders of the martyrs of the Civil Rights movement and I want to offer my wholehearted thanks and appreciation for your incredible contribution.

It's the power to believe that you see—you visualize a sense of community, a sense of family, and a sense of one house. We didn't have a computer or even a fax machine, but we used what we had. We had the weapons of truth and justice. And we had ourselves, so we put our bodies on the line to make a difference in our society. We were just ordinary people with extraordinary vision, imbued with the discipline and philosophy of nonviolence.

We have come a great distance in just a few decades, but we still have a distance to go before we build the Beloved Community. Your legacy of strong, inclusive leadership continues through all of the incredible lives you have touched over the years. I am so grateful to be a part of this momentous collection, even in a small way.

Again, I want to thank you for not being quiet but for having the power and courage to stand up. Please accept my sincere thanks for everything you have done to build a better future for our young people. You are a dear friend and an example to us all.

Sincerely,
John Lewis
Member of Congress

Steve Suitts

FEBRUARY 29, 2016

Dear Leslie,

Recently I decided that I wanted to write you a letter as my way of joining others in expressing my deep appreciation and admiration for the life you have led and the contributions you have made to the South and the nation. A letter is decidedly old-school in this era of electronic communications and emoticons and, therefore, is the more fitting means for me to convey a few thoughts to someone who is, in my mind, an old-school Southern liberal.

I can already see in my mind's eye your face shifting into an expression of cautious puzzlement about being called an "old-school Southern liberal." My hunch is that you can see my point about the "Southern liberal." You have never shied away from that identity, and, even when you were camped up North for more than 20 years, you could not be anything more or less than a Southerner. That fact alone would justify my term for you. I doubt there are very many folk who have lived all their lives in the South today and who self-identify as a Southerner first and foremost.

Your liberalism is well documented in your own writing. I think I have read every book you have published, and all have in one way or another echoed themes of your *Republic of Equals,* an essential argument for the equality of humankind in the context of the interracial South. Your book, *Common Interests,* which also sits on my book shelf, demonstrated how your understanding of the enemies of equality had evolved as the South and the nation changed from 1967 to 1988. I'm not certain that you would have approved of this statement, if one of your students in a political science course at Emory nearly 60 years ago had made it, but your unrelenting words over many decades insisting that state and federal policies must combat effectively racism, poverty, and militarism constitute the strongest evidence of your intellectual leadership as a Southern liberal who will not allow the fashion of the times to alter his analysis.

Oddly enough, I remember that one of your oral histories done almost 40 years ago at Chapel Hill started out by your saying something like "I'm not someone who has great, unusually dramatic things happen to him." Perhaps, so. But, what your declaration obscures is the fact that you helped to enable some dramatic things. You helped to start the Voter Education Project and insured its funding for many years as it enabled a majority of black Southerners to become voting citizens. You supported the opportunity and right of black communities to start and control in the South key institutions (such as farmers coops, day care centers and Head Start centers, credit unions, etc.). You were perhaps the first in the world of organized philanthropy to recognize and support the Native American Rights Movement. You were among the first in that world to support the farmer workers movement. And much more.

After I arrived and settled into the job of executive director of the Southern Regional Council (SRC) in July, 1977, I looked back and thought a good deal about my predecessors, beginning with Will Alexander and the Commission on Interracial Cooperation and running through George Esser. There were many financial problems at SRC at that time (I still have a copy of the page from the 1977 audit showing that SRC had a net worth of $64,000 at the end of that year.), but I believed that any recovery of the organization would depend on how well I created an intellectual framework for people's understanding of SRC's vital role in addressing the major issues of the South and nation and how well I could make some "dramatic things happen" with little money and time.

As you may recall, you did not support my appointment as SRC director and I think it is fair to say that during my early years at SRC, you did not believe I could succeed in bringing the organization back to a vital role. (Yes, this is not the first time I have reminded you of these facts since you left the Field Foundation.) The irony, however, is that I came to understand what I had to do at SRC and I found my best model for the way to do it in your own past leadership. I was partial to George Mitchell's dry humor and language, which framed issues in the context of striving for a "democratic South," but it was your intellectual power and rigor in the cause of making "dramatic things happen" that gave me the model I tried to follow more than any other.

And it has been your example of combining rigorous scholarship in direct or indirect support of effective activism that I have found myself following over the years. Whenever I have told young people who are eager to change the South and the world that effective activism involves some of the most challenging intellectual work they will ever do, I have more than once used you as my case in point.

I am pleased that our friendship grew over the years, and I hope that you will remember it as something that has been of some value to you. I know that I have considered it as something of great value. Still, I do not think I ever told you how much your own life of scholarship and activism has influenced my own. Now I have—even if far, far overdue.

When I was working at SRC to produce the radio documentary, "Will the Circle Be Unbroken," we came up with this notion of describing many local activists in what modern scholars now call the long civil rights movement: "ordinary people who did extraordinary things." It was a term that generally fit. But, there also were, in that time and since then, some extraordinary people who have done extraordinary things. Some are well-known in popular culture, and some are not.

For the record, you were among those extraordinary people who have done extraordinary things. I am grateful that you did them because, in James McBride Dabbs's old-school phrasing, you loved the South so much you wanted to make it better. And, most of all, I am grateful to have counted you as my friend.

My best, now as always.

Your friend,

Steve Suitts

A Short Biography

Leslie W. Dunbar was with the Atlanta-based Southern Regional Council during the tumultuous days of the civil rights movement, as its director of research (1958 to 1960) and its Executive Director (1961 to 1965). He was a passionate voice for acknowledging and following the black leadership of the southern struggle. With SCLC's Martin Luther King, Jr., and the NAACP's Roy Wilkins, he helped to organize the Voter Education Project, and sponsored it within the Southern Regional Council. Under the direction of Wiley A. Branton and Mr. Dunbar's once-assistant, Vernon E. Jordan, Jr., the Voter Education Project is credited with registering two million African American voters in the 1960's.

His emphasis was funding local projects, not national groups. He was a guest at the signing of the Voting Rights Act at the White House in 1965.

Leslie is a native of Greenbrier County, West Virginia. His family was an early victim of the Great Depression and left the Greenbrier Valley for Baltimore, where he attended public schools including the University of Maryland. When the war came he supervised the assembly of B-26 bombers at the Glenn L. Martin aircraft plant. Without a college degree he was admitted to Cornell University for graduate studies in political philosophy and Constitutional law. After teaching political science at Emory University, he moved to the Atomic Energy Commission in 1951 as Chief of Community Affairs, overseeing the sudden influx of workers and scientists to the Aiken, South Carolina, area as the AEC's immense Savannah River Plant was brought online. He returned to academia to teach at Mount Holyoke in Massachusetts, where he chaired the political science department.

But he answered his true calling, motivated by what he called

"Southern-born common sense," and retuned to Atlanta in 1958 to join the staff of the Southern Regional Council. "It was a time of mind-changing in the South," he said, "and SRC was central to that." After guiding the SRC into the storm of civil rights as the forum for "people of good will," Mr. Dunbar moved with his family to New York in 1965 to direct the Field Foundation, a philanthropy founded by the Chicago department store family and dedicated to child welfare and civil rights. In that role, until 1980, he championed (and funded) the existence of the Friends of the Children Head Start program in Mississippi in the face of state efforts to eradicate the program. He steered Field Foundation funds to provide substantial, probably primary, support for Martin Luther King's Poor People's Campaign, which continued through organizational difficulties after Dr. King's assassination. He was instrumental in providing financial sustenance to the fledgling Children's Defense Fund under the direction of Marian Wright Edelman. He was an early supporter of Cesar Chavez's United Farm Workers' Association, and of La Raza, a leading Latino advocacy organization, which in recent years has enjoyed the support of Michelle Obama. While he was content with his role in the background, the proper position, he believed, for white Southerners in the civil rights struggle, he was once escorted by the Capitol police, in a dignified way, from a sit-in at the House of Representatives protesting funding for the War in Viet Nam.

He was a "scholar-at-large" with the United Negro College Fund in 1984–1985, and taught at Shaw University in Raleigh and Xavier University in New Orleans. His working career concluded at the Ford Foundation, studying poverty in a project he privately concluded to be extravagantly expensive, but which did result in the publication of his book, *Minority Rights, What Has Happened to Blacks, Hispanics, American Indians & Other Minorities in the Eighties*. This was one of a large collection of books he wrote, one of the last being *Looking for the Future, A Meditation on Political Choice*, a commentary on American militarism and democracy published in 2012 when he was 91.

"Retiring" to Durham, North Carolina, and well into his seventies, Leslie became a volunteer in the "guardian ad litem" program and narrowly lost a campaign for election to the Durham School Board. He became active in the social justice ministry of the Watts Street Baptist Church, and in 1992, along with its pastor, the Reverend Mel Williams, founded the Religious Coalition for a Nonviolent Durham.

Long a passionate critic of "Southern Congressmen," and later "Republican Congressmen" in general, he has maintained his commitment to dozens of grassroots civil rights, labor, and political groups, and lives now in New Orleans, Louisiana.

A Leslie Dunbar Reader

A Republic of Equals, The University of Michigan, 1966. ("This is not a book about civil rights, about the Negro revolt, or about the South.")

Minority Report, What Has Happened to Blacks, Hispanics, American Indians, & Other Minorities in the Eighties, [edited by Leslie W. Dunbar], Pantheon Books, 1984. ("The United States has been wrestling with its 'minority question' nearly as long as our history itself has run.")

The Common Interest, How Our Social-Welfare Policies Don't Work, and What We Can Do About Them, Pantheon Books, 1988. ("Social-welfare policies are about human beings. They are about the national interest also, if anyone can distinguish between the two.")

Reclaiming Liberalism, W. W. Norton & Company, 1991. ("The invasion of Panama was no different essentially from other recent American aggressions.")

The Shame of Southern Politics, Essays and Speeches, The University Press of Kentucky, 2002. ("I would like to claim for this book, despite its many mistaken analyses and so much of importance being left out, that it is nevertheless true to the spirit of the citizen reform movements of the late 1950s, the 1960s, and the 1970s, and that it grasps some portion of their essential features.")

Where We Stand, Voices of Southern Dissent [Leslie Dunbar, contributor], NewSouth Books, 2004. ("Our Imperiled Union! I say imperiled not from apprehension of an external threat or even overt repudiation of the Constitution, but from belief that the Bush II Administration, in succession of others dating back to the war against the Vietnamese, yet outreaching all, is embedding in our polity principles transformative of the republic.")

American Crisis, Southern Solutions: From Where We Stand, Promise and Peril [Leslie W. Dunbar, contributor], NewSouth Books, 2008. ("Since the 2006 congressional elections, Democrats have looked forward hungrily to 2008.")

Looking For The Future: A Meditation on Political Choice, NewSouth Books, 2012. ("I have lived most of my life up and down and sideways in our Eastern states and reside now in the venerable city of New Orleans on Magazine Street, so-called because its one-time French occupiers used its buildings as warehouses, especially for exports, which is still a recognizable English meaning of 'magazines'.")

As the South Lies Dying, Its Dueling Legacies: A Selection of Essays, 2014. ("For most of humanity's poor and discarded, change —real, useful social change—is as elusive, and as seductive, as the Holy Grail.")

www.ingramcontent.com/pod-product-compliance
Lightning Source LLC
LaVergne TN
LVHW091320080426
835510LV00007B/569